POLLINATOR PALS

BETH THE BUTTERFLY POLLINATES

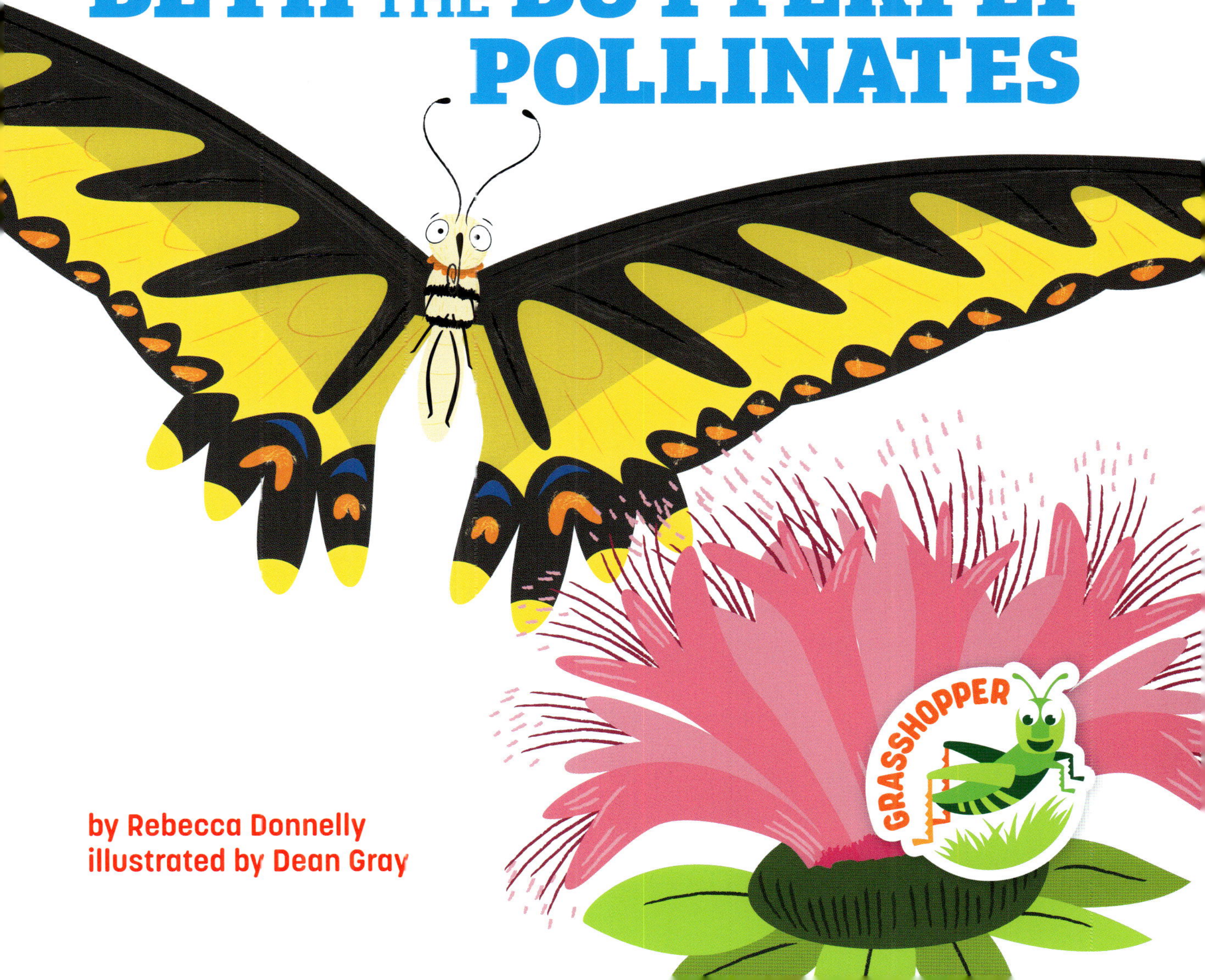

by Rebecca Donnelly
illustrated by Dean Gray

Tools for Parents & Teachers

Grasshopper Books enhance imagination and introduce the earliest readers to fiction with fun storylines and illustrations. The easy-to-read text supports early reading experiences with repetitive sentence patterns and sight words.

Before Reading

- Discuss the cover illustration. What do they see?
- Look at the glossary together. Discuss the words.

Read the Book

- Read the book to the child, or have him or her read independently.
- "Walk" through the book and look at the illustrations. Who is the main character? What is happening in the story?

After Reading

- Prompt the child to think more. Ask: Have you ever seen a butterfly? What was it doing?

Grasshopper Books are published by Jump!
5357 Penn Avenue South
Minneapolis, MN 55419
www.jumplibrary.com

Library of Congress Cataloging-in-Publication Data

Names: Donnelly, Rebecca, author.
Gray, Dean, illustrator.
Title: Beth the butterfly pollinates / by Rebecca Donnelly; illustrated by Dean Gray.
Description: Minneapolis, MN: Jump!, Inc., [2022]
Series: Pollinator pals
Includes reading tips and supplementary back matter.
Audience: Ages 7-10.
Identifiers: LCCN 2021000101 (print)
LCCN 2021000102 (ebook)
ISBN 9781636902258 (hardcover)
ISBN 9781636902265 (paperback)
ISBN 9781636902272 (ebook)
Subjects: LCSH: Readers (Primary)
Papilionidae–Juvenile fiction.
Classification: LCC PE1119.2 .D67 2022 (print)
LCC PE1119.2 (ebook)
DDC 428.6/2–dc23
LC record available at https://lccn.loc.gov/2021000101
LC ebook record available at https://lccn.loc.gov/2021000102

Editor: Eliza Leahy
Direction and Layout: Anna Peterson
Illustrator: Dean Gray

Printed in the United States of America at Corporate Graphics in North Mankato, Minnesota.

Table of Contents

Sunshine and Flowers

Hello! I'm Beth. I am a swallowtail caterpillar. I live in a garden full of flowers and vegetables.

It's time for me to make a chrysalis. While inside, I will turn into a butterfly. It is called metamorphosis. See you soon!

Here I am! I spent two weeks inside my chrysalis. Now I am a butterfly! I have wings. I fly around and look for food.

I get all the nutrients I need from flower nectar. Big, bright wildflowers are my favorite. Red flowers are very tasty. I love carrot and mint plants, too.

mint plant
carrot plant

This looks like a good place to eat! I start to land.

Oh, no! There is a praying mantis. They love to eat butterflies. I quickly fly away.

praying
mantis

Look, more flowers!
I don't see any predators.
I will be safe here.

I can taste with my feet! When I land on a leaf or flower, taste buds on my feet and legs tell me what kind of plant I am on. I'm looking for plants with lots of yummy nectar inside.

I have a long proboscis. It uncurls. I can reach into flowers that have nectar deep inside. Like a straw, it helps me drink. Yum!

When I reach into a blossom, pollen sticks to me. When I fly to another flower, I leave some pollen on it. That is how I pollinate! Now this flower can make seeds. New plants can grow.

pollen

Here's my friend Mona.
She is a monarch butterfly.

Mona loves this garden, too. With lots of wildflowers around, butterflies have plenty to eat!

I am cold-blooded. I need warmth from the sun to move. When the sun goes down, I rest in this tree. In the morning, I will visit more flowers and spread more pollen. Sweet dreams!

Let's Review!

How do butterflies pollinate flowering plants and garden vegetables? Take a look at Beth's journey!

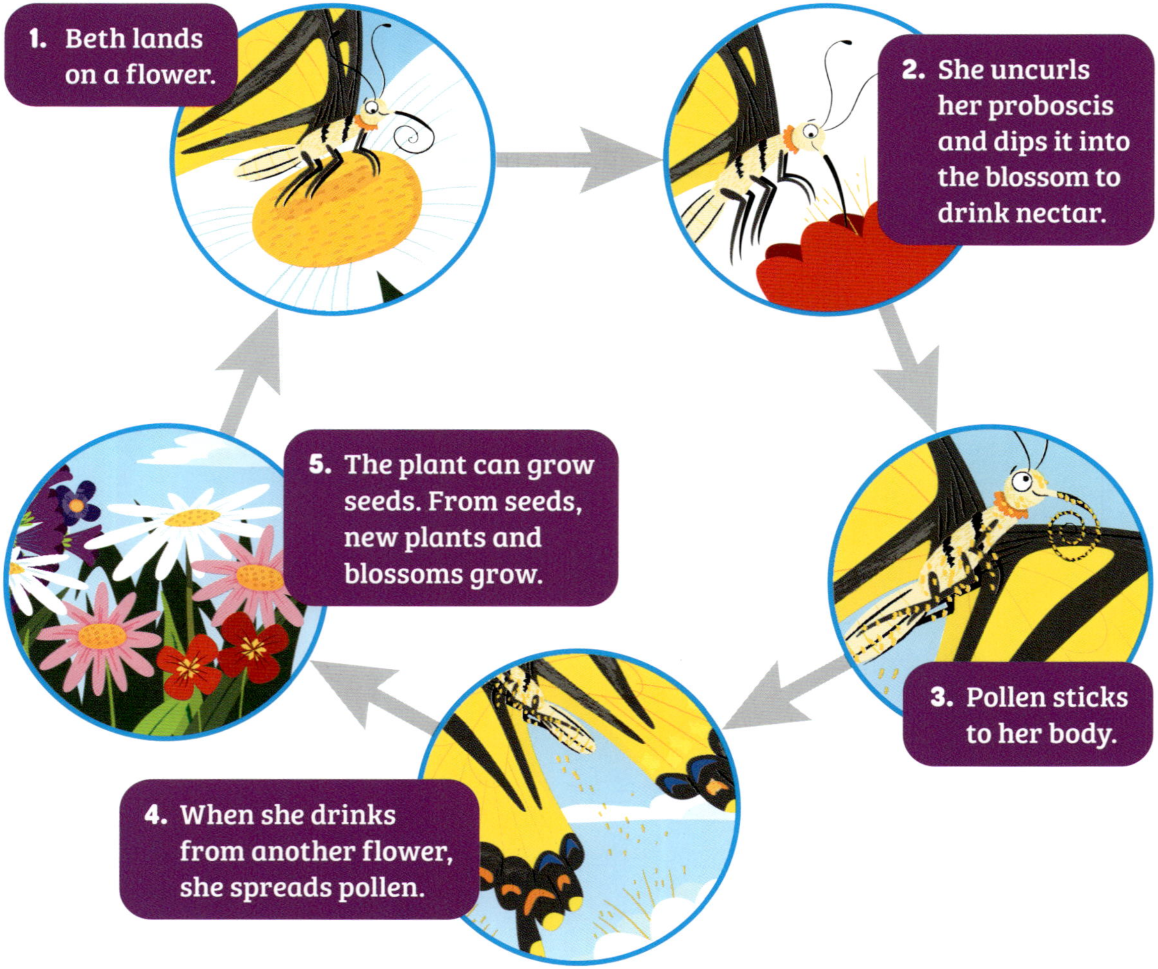

Where Eastern Tiger Swallowtails Live

Beth is an eastern tiger swallowtail butterfly. These butterflies live in the eastern part of North America. Take a look!

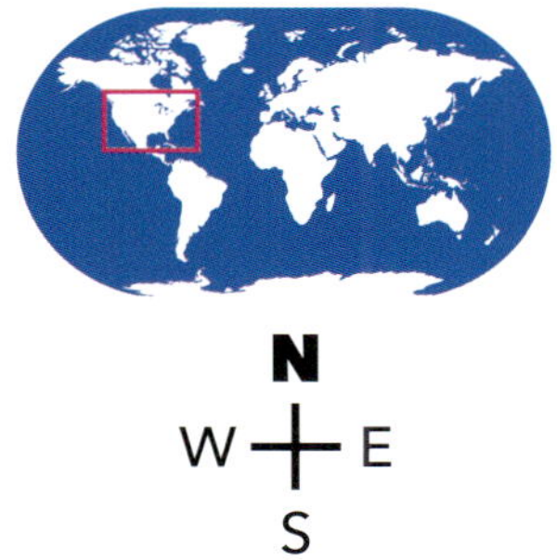

To Learn More

Finding more information is as easy as 1, 2, 3.

FACT SURFER

1. Go to www.factsurfer.com
2. Enter "**Baththebutterflypollinates**" into the search box.
3. Choose your book to see a list of websites.

Glossary

blossom: A flower on a tree or bush.

chrysalis: The hard shell that protects a caterpillar as it turns into an adult butterfly.

cold-blooded: Needing heat from a source like the sun to stay warm.

metamorphosis: A series of changes caterpillars go through as they develop into adults.

nectar: A sweet liquid made by flowers to attract pollinators.

nutrients: Substances, such as proteins, minerals, or vitamins, that are needed by plants, animals, and people to stay healthy.

pollen: A powder made by the male parts of plants.

pollinate: To take pollen from the male part of a flower and put it on the female part of a flower so the plant can reproduce.

predators: Animals that hunt other animals for food.

proboscis: A tubelike mouthpart that is used to suck nectar.

taste buds: Groups of cells that sense whether something is sweet, sour, salty, or bitter.

Index